TIBET

Flammarion

photography **YANN ROMAIN**   text **HIPPOLYTE ROMAIN**

STYLE

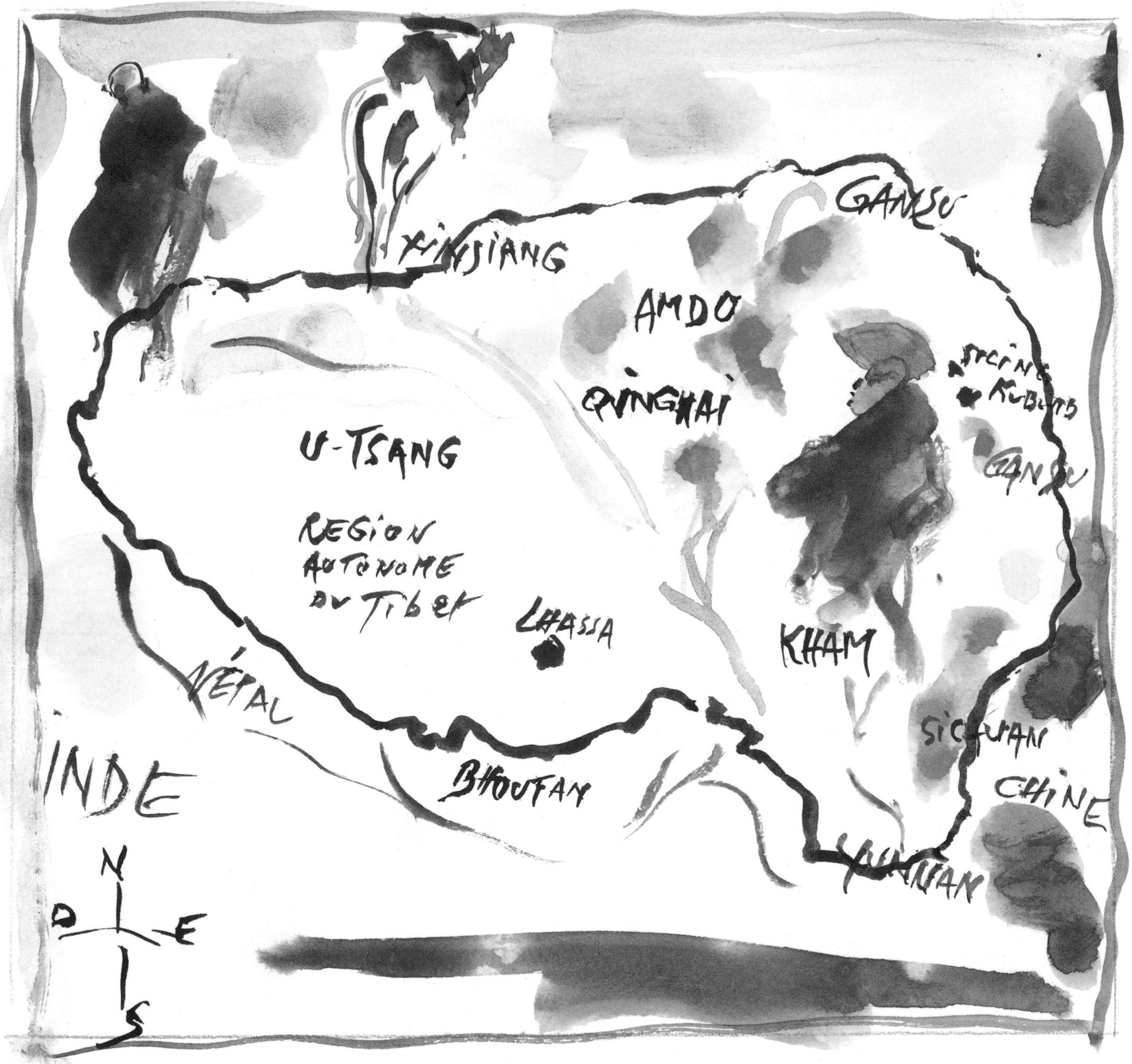

XINJIANG

GANSU

AMDO

QINGHAI

U-TSANG

REGION
AUTONOME
DU TIBET

STEING
KOUKOU

GANSU

KHAM

LHASSA

NÉPAL

BHOUTAN

SICHUAN

CHINE

YUNNAN

INDE

N
O   E
S

4

✝ ✝

I should say from the outset that this is a story told by a traveler in love with Tibet; it simply describes what I have observed in the region of Amdo, where these photographs were taken. I am by no means attempting to discuss the entire country, a huge land where the differences between the inhabitants of Lhasa, Xinjiang, Qinghai, and Gansu are great. Many such accounts date from anytime between 1980 and 2000, but things change quickly, and in these lands the transformations and adaptations that occur are so extraordinary that a decade can encompass two or three times as much. Thus, my story concerns the year 2005; I cannot speak for the future.

Northeastern Tibet, a religious place, is also deeply nomadic as its social and ethnic fabric is made up of numerous tribes. Tibetan Buddhism seems to predominate, but the entire Hui Muslim community—who own almost all the businesses in this region—practice a non-radical form of Islam. In any case, social structures have left the younger generation of Hui ill-educated and, since they are introduced into commerce at a very early age, their principal source of education is the mosque and the Imam in charge. Around 300 million Muslims and as many Buddhists can be found in China; and even in Tibet, in a town in the Amdo province of thirty thousand souls, for example, one can find fifteen brand-new, well-frequented mosques.

We cannot fail to be struck by the concentrated and devout human tide, when on Fridays, the day of prayer, we find ourselves in the middle of a crowd of bearded men, all dressed similarly in long black coats, and their heads covered by little white skullcaps. All the storefronts are adorned with Arabic writing, and even if the majority of the inhabitants speak Chinese, Arabic and Tibetan are also very common. Xining, like the majority of the urban areas, is archetypical of new Chinese towns: tainted by flashy modernity, with its facades illuminated by garish neon signs, and encircled by mass urbanism, a mix of sinister housing projects—often in an advanced state of dilapidation—and mushrooming new constructions. These are the signs of an era of triumphant capitalism, but they are hardly more attractive, just more recent. Glass hotel buildings plastered with posters declaring luxury and prosperity stand alongside concrete cubes built to house the newly emerging middle classes; all this against a backdrop of anarchic traffic, where sedan automobiles have taken over from bicycles. Dust, dirt, and depressing pseudo-luxury come together in a continual din, with occasional power cuts that can last several hours—the result of a lack of sufficient energy supplies. And in the midst of this social upheaval, one finds the resignation of the everyman, powerless to assess any kind of ideology or critique of this new order. Only one thought dominates in everyone's mind: get rich quick and think of nothing else.

So, keep this brief sketch of today's Chinese Tibet in mind while I take you several hundred miles away, through the mountain passes ascending 11,500 feet (3,500 m), towards Kumbum, Labrang, and Xiahe. This world is nearby yet very different; a world that has had to assimilate the indispensable cell phone, the reconstruction of the monasteries, the monastic life of certain members and the charlatanism of others. Here, we no longer speak of towns, but of villages. The sacrosanct protection of concrete has gone and we enter a world of nomads, holy men, desperados, occupying Chinese militia, and wide-open spaces where rules and laws are often ill-defined. One discovers both the beauty and squalidness

of Tibetan families in the streets of Kumbum, where grubby children—real angels with dirty faces—wander aimlessly. Independence, brutality, nobility, strength, cunning: such are the attributes of the Tibetans that one meets in the markets of Kumbum. And to disarm you further, they wear broad smiles and a perpetually roguish air. The girls are like mountain gypsies: beautiful, proud, and inaccessible; their grandmothers are like small wrinkled apples. Trailing behind the women's handmade boots are swarms of mischievous urchins; the men assume an air of weary yet elegant dignity. These are the nomads. Their caravans consist of tents, and their wealth lies in the flocks of sheep grazing in villages that are snowed up for eight months of the year, villages that resemble those towns of the Wild West with one main street lined with stores and market stalls, beyond which lies nothing—here, just the mountains. The traffic comprises dusty trucks, motorcycles, horses, broken-down automobiles; the pedestrians are monks clad in red—claret, crimson, pink, or scarlet—and Tibetan peasants, each of whom drifts along taking an interest in everything, a dagger in his belt and a savage look on his face.

This region is intersected by a winding road which ascends, descends, and meanders interminably through the hills and valleys. Often there is a precipice or ditch on either side; an occasional tiny village made up of a few stone-and-wood two-story houses springs up from out of nowhere. On the outskirts, donkeys and dogs roam freely, indifferent to the weather and the seasons. The wind gusts constantly, blowing up clumps of snow in winter, or sand and dust in summer. Everything is ocher, and perturbing tar-black clouds can fill the pure azure sky in a few minutes. But the overwhelming first impression for a traveler in these lands is still the space—a great emptiness where the elements dominate to such an extent that

✝✝✝✝✝✝✝✝✝✝✝✝✝✝✝✝✝✝✝✝✝✝✝✝✝

humans, in their helplessness, feel naturally inclined to seek a sense of complicity, spirituality, and modesty in the face of this exceptional nature, both disturbing and grandiose in its majesty.

The Tibet portrayed in this book is little known, lying on the Mongolian border, 1,243 miles (2,000 km) north of Lhasa. In the regions of Kham and Amdo live nomads, most of whom are herdsmen. The population is made up of many different ethnicities such as the Muslim Hui, the Tu, and various others—all Tibetan. The areas situated at altitudes of over 9,900 feet (3,000 m) are battered by the wind, are covered with snow in winter and endure scorching summers in their mountain pastures. We are far from the Potala Palace and Lhasa, the capital of the Tibet Autonomous Region, which lies close to Nepal and Bhutan.

Many of these nomads venerate His Holiness the Dalai Lama, but the Panchen Lama also has an important status. The influence of the monasteries, of the reincarnations of the living Buddha and a whole complex hierarchy closely based on a medieval model makes the relationship between temporal power and spiritual power difficult. Certain monasteries resemble fortresses, encircled below by the monks' houses and further downhill by the village where the ordinary trading folk live. For these proud horsemen, the inhabitants of the southern capital have allowed themselves to be corrupted by the consumerism imported from China. But how can we pass judgment on this lost young generation, whose material preoccupations have become their creed, and whose spiritual guide left the country half a century ago? For too long, tourists—consumers of ideologies as well as products—have hoped to find in Tibet a sort of original purity imbued with spirituality.

A land of monks and novices flying kites and practicing archery in monastery courtyards; these incredibly beautiful images have been continually rehashed over the years, totally obscuring the reality as if these men and women emerged from a different mold than the rest of us. We see them as our deliverers, as gentle savages turned holy men, praying and counting their prayer beads to redeem our human frailties.

If Tibetans are fundamentally religious, it is because nature is hostile and the part of Tibetan Buddhism that emerged from the Bön religion remains very close to pagan cults. Gods, Buddhas, and reincarnations make up a very simple way of life, providing ordinary individuals with glimpses of the divine. But theft, jealousy, lies, envy, and all the deadly sins held dear by Judeo-Christians are shared by the Tibetans. They are mortal: Karma allows one either to atone for past errors or to improve future lives.

Today, the horsemen ride motorbikes, and the girls do not seem to notice the difference or have any problem with it. Everyone owns a cell phone and flirtation is still a prime occupation for the young; you only have to watch them parading in the villages during the Tibetan New Year celebrations. The boys wear designer sunglasses, leather pants, and their heavy sheepskin coats are trimmed with speckled fur to show how well-off they are. These pelisses—which function just like portable shelters—are handed down from father to son, and when the temperature drops to twenty-two degrees below zero (-30°C), they are responsible for saving many a man's life. The girls, with their sunburned cheeks, braid their long hair and cover themselves with chased silver jewelry studded with hard stones. It is like an unending "Court of Love," where each girl smiles, turns, and walks past nonchalantly with a brazen look, in search of compliments. The girls accept their beauty and desire to please without false modesty, but when a suitor becomes too insistent or forces a compliment, they blush to the roots of their hair and run off laughing. At the same time, in the backrooms of the Muslim stores, novice monks are glued to computer consoles, playing war games and, through bursts of laughter, casually massacring anything that moves on the screen.

Often at night, when the cold outside the pothouses is harsh enough to break stones, the monks sit huddled in the folds of their heavy crimson coats for hours, seemingly waiting for some unidentified passerby. These immobile, almost disquieting shadows are guarding against unknown evil spirits.

This is northern Tibet, the Tibet of noble brigands, and this book is dedicated to its nomadic beauty which is paraded defiantly, like an anthem to freedom.

The different tribes that compose the population of Tibet have each contributed to the creation of a nomadic world enhanced by Turkish, Mongolian, Indian, Nepalese, Chinese, and sometimes Western influences. This is the result of many invasions over the centuries, but it is also due to the caravans that plied the "Silk Road" and which were robbed regularly by the *campas*, the noble brigands of Amdo and Kham. This has resulted in a true Tibetan aesthetic, both rich and baroque but also possessing a symbolic quality: transforming holy objects into jewelry out of a desire to show off and be original, but equally to mark oneself out and parade one's differences in a religious world dominated by lamas.

Nomadic clothing displays the gamut of reds enriched with gold and "burnt-yellow" belonging to the Buddhist monks. Fox, wolf, wild dog, and snow leopard furs, as well as printed fabrics, echo the patterns of these animals, whose images are linked to such qualities as strength, cunning, power, and even courage; mixed together they become a lining or decoration for the sleeve, the collar, or the bottom edge of a coat.

✝ ✝

This fashion is a form of elegance, at once rough-and-ready and completely organized: scraps are used as patches to repair tears and layering is justified by the extreme cold. The seeming anarchy which emerges from these different materials is intended and demonstrates that this baroque fashion is functional as well as providing a means of recognizing the social class of particular men and women. Accessories are piled on, from belts accented with silver to necklaces weighed down with ivory, not to mention the incredible earrings adorned with hard stones. The mystical beauty of their bracelets, rings, and prayer beads (*malas*) is often the result of a kind of ethnic alchemy that mixes the sacred with the profane; the personal touches are apparent in the addition of amulets, strips of ribbon, and scraps of sacred cloth.

The heavy sheepskin coats edged with fur and embroidered fabric are essentials, since they are genuine miniature portable tents to counter the icy winter temperatures. But they are also an aesthetic choice, the result of careful thought and great expense—such a pelisse costs the equivalent of three or four yaks.

Finally, there is the manner in which these clothes are worn, and here, too, the nomads demonstrate their taste for freedom and their simple but true spirituality. The Tibetan people face life head-on, confronting the skies and the winds, talking to the mountains, the stars, and all the gods who rule the destinies of men.

In this world of gods and foreordained destinies, Yann Romain did not encounter these nomads and holy men by chance. Chance does not exist: Yann Romain has simply reconnected the threads of previous lives. You can doubt, mock, shrug your shoulders, or refute these feelings, reducing them to nonsense, but it remains true that in this place his encounters with a living Buddha, with nomadic families, and his friendships in a large number of villages and monasteries have made him a privileged explorer. His camera lens is no longer a voyeuristic object but rather a third eye; a sort of oil lamp lighting the path ahead, where his images embody words full of affection for the villagers. For fifteen years, Romain was a society and fashion photographer for glossy magazines and it was his taste for clothes and beauty that attracted him to these tribes, where the women adorn themselves with jewels for the festivities and the men parade around like dudes. The elderly and the children—the former wrinkled and wise, the latter little street urchins elegantly dressed up "nomad-style," the acme of the ragpicker's art—have secured him to this world forever. The love of Romain's life is a young Tibetan called De Qin, and even if this book is not exactly a wedding gift, it will remain for many Amdo families a testimony of their life in the twenty-first century, where adaptation is all but where the Tibetans have understood that only flexibility and intelligence will enable them to preserve their culture.

TIBETAN
ELEGANCE

✛ ✛ ✛ ✛ ✛ ✛ ✛ ✛ ✛ ✛ ✛ ✛ ✛ ✛

For centuries, caravans have transported precious objects across mountains and deserts. Whether from eastern Turkey and the Middle East or from northern Tartary and Mongolia, Tibetans—nomadic shepherds and noble brigands alike—are always adorned with necklaces, rings, and belts decorated with silver and hard stones. Beauty and appearance are highly prized in this world where travel and spirituality reign. The women adore dressing up and showing off the wealth of their family or clan. Depending on the tribe, specific meanings are associated with this earring or those prayer beads. Silver, ivory, coral, and turquoise are the noble materials that decorate the Tibetan world.

OM MANI PEME HUNG They are proud men and their nomadic elegance reveals that clothing constitutes almost everything for them: a home, a suit of armor, and a distinctive social indicator. Muffled figures wander in the cold at an altitude of 11,500 feet (3,500 m); it is just five degrees (-15°C) and the wind gusts clouds of sand and dust.

TIBETAN ELEGANCE

As hunters and herdsmen primarily, the peoples of Tibet have always appreciated fur: firstly, because of the extreme cold that prevails for eight months of the year on the high plateaus of Amdo and the Himalayas, but also because the conventions of the herdsmen and the ruling classes demand the display of as much wealth as possible. Monks might only keep a strict minimum of possessions—of vegetable origin, as Buddhism forbids the destruction of any animal life—but ordinary nomads venerate the snow leopard, the wolf, and the fox, and are proud to wear these skins as proof of their courage and freedom.

Sunglasses have always been an indispensable accessory in the life of Tibetans, whether they are mountain guides, Sherpas, or simply shepherds. At these high altitudes, the snow glare is such that it would be pure madness not to protect one's eyes. In matters of eyewear fashion, the influence of the emperors, well accustomed to living alongside Chinese and Muslim traders, has long been a determining factor. Large round lenses like portholes and gilded frames with articulated arms dominate the market. Today, more and more Western brands are winning over followers, and dandies must flaunt the very latest style in shades if they are to seduce the girls who are so fond of Western trends.

✝ ✝ ✝ ✝ ✝ ✝ ✝ ✝ ✝ ✝ ✝ ✝ ✝ ✝ ✝

The predilection for exhibitionism and the desire to seduce do not diminish with age. During the huge get-togethers for the summer solstice, the moon festival, and the turn of the new year, everyone feels compelled to show off his wealth and, above all, to prove his love for life and demonstrate his thanks to Buddha and the protecting gods—both for all the years gone by and for the future, which hopefully will be even better.

Tibet. A magical but troubling word that evokes so many things: the silhouettes of monks draped in crimson; the spirituality of Buddhism; images of the Dalai Lama; imposing prayer wheels in sculpted wood turned tirelessly by pilgrims as they pass in front of the monasteries; smells of rancid butter burning in the oil lamps and incense fumes rising around the gilded, smiling buddhas. But behind these picture-postcard images, what do we know of the men and women who live in the mountains and valleys of this huge land?

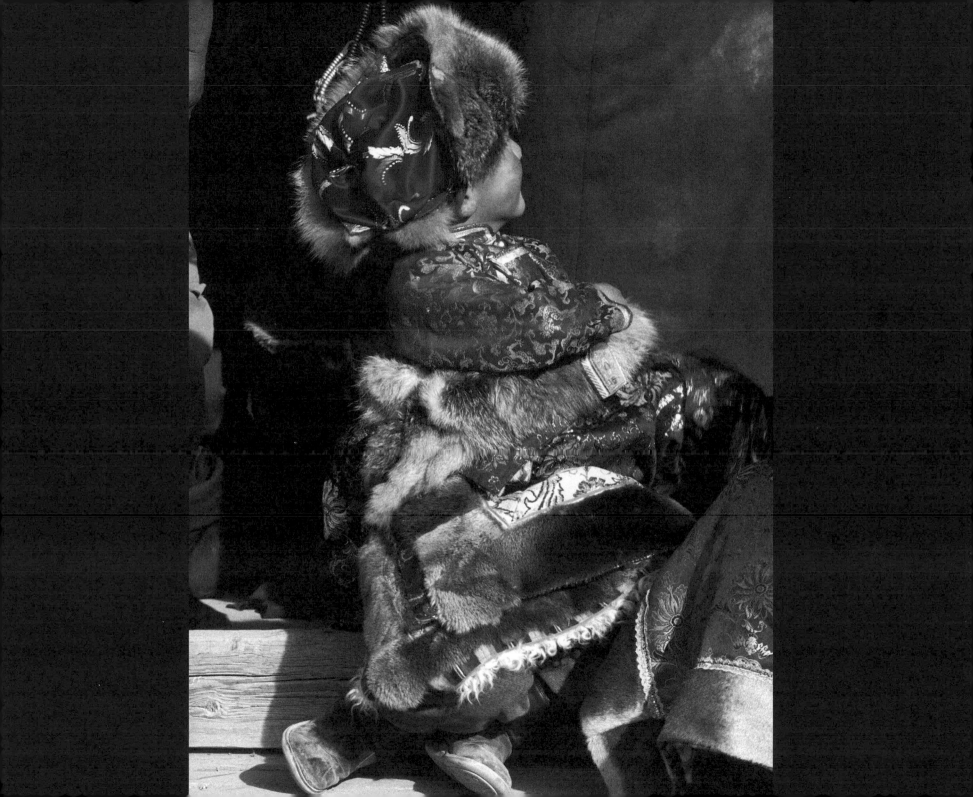

✝
✝
✝
✝ | **OM MANI PEME HUNG** The children are urchins of the steppes. Long-haired and dirty, with insolent smiles and eyes that sparkle with malice, they are angelic popinjays dressed in patched-up sheepskin and hats larger than the immense prayer wheels that turn in the monasteries.

NOMADIC
ENCOUNTERS

✛
✛
✛
✛

OM MANI PEME HUNG The soul of the nomad has not changed, and even if the motorcycle has replaced the horse, what does it matter? Tibet is not a picture-postcard idyll for Westerners in need of spirituality. Life is harsh and often brutish on these high plateaus; nature defends itself and the gods are sometimes forgetful. But the future lies in education, adaptation, and hope.

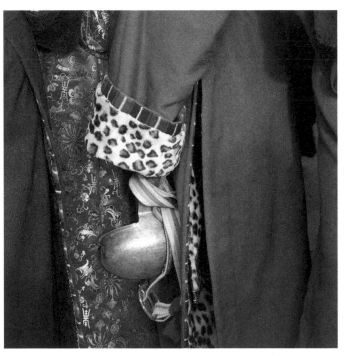

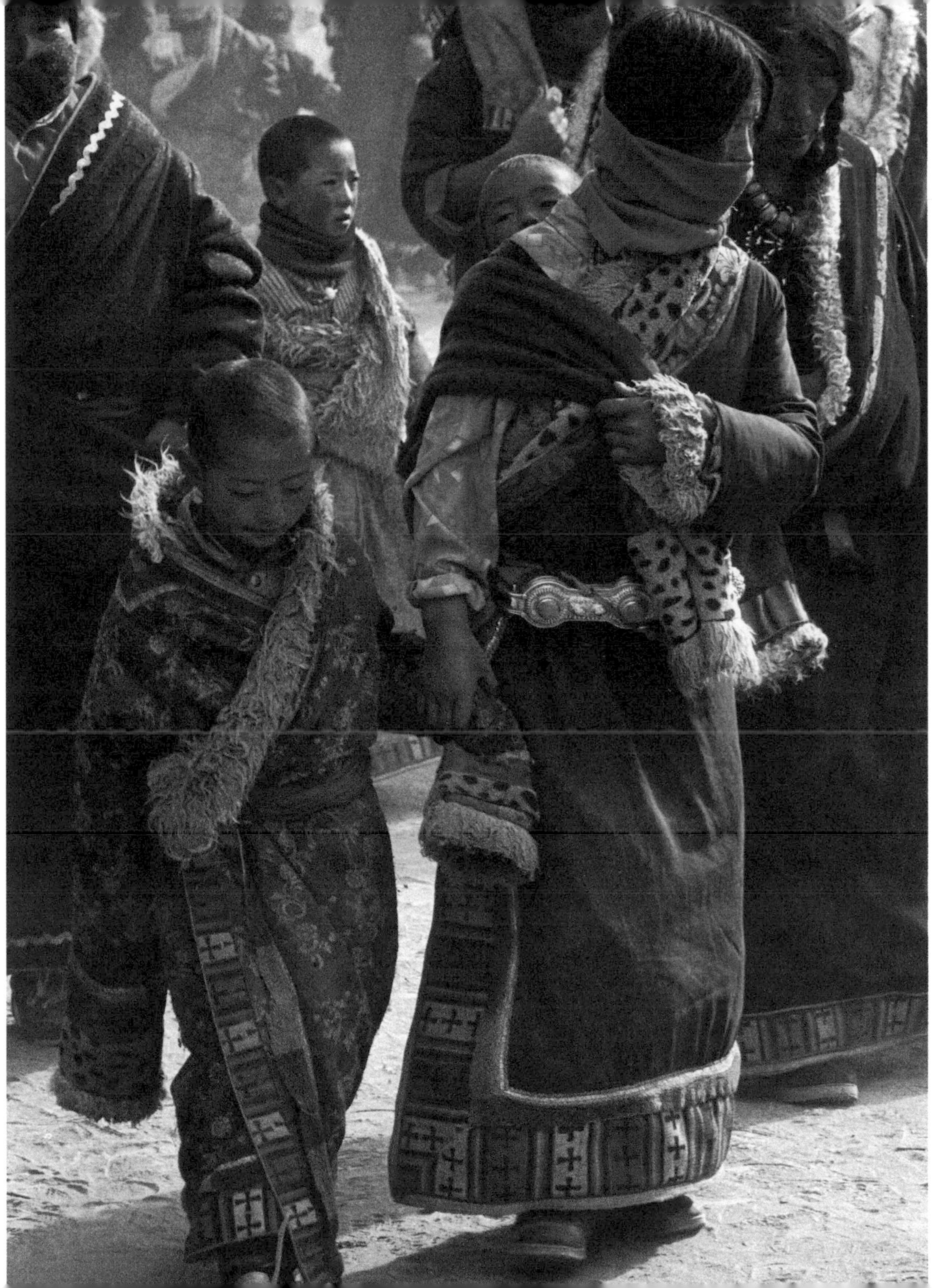

✛
✛
✛
✛

OM MANI PEME HUNG The electric guitar and drum kit have arrived, but the girls of Amdo continue to dance and sing like their mothers—only now it takes place in front of a karaoke screen.

During the Enlightenment period, in the reign of Emperor Kangxi, a high-ranking mandarin—his hat adorned with peacock feathers and jade—traveled as an ambassador to the distant lands of northern Tibet. For some time, he had heard a rumor which had doubtless been exaggerated by the word-of-mouth stories spread by gossips and the inventive imagination of nomads. The rumor recounted to anyone who would listen that a young, extremely beautiful novice monk held court in matters of love and philosophy just an arrow-flight's distance from the monastery of Labrang. Because of his great wisdom, and thanks both to his network of devoted informers and his paid spies, nothing escaped the notice of the Emperor, and he demanded a detailed report on this strange affair as soon as possible.

Lost in the heart of the mountains in the Amdo region, the village of Xining, which lay at the foot of a fortress, was completely unremarkable except for its inn, where merchants and a few savage brigands would take restorative meals of noodle soup, black tea, and smoked yak. It was also known for its competition of verbal jousting, held twice a year, which gave a monk or a run-of-the-mill yarn-spinner the opportunity of winning two tea bricks. Never in the memory of the villagers had a Chinese person taken part in this kind of spectacle.

When the mandarin's advance party arrived and requisitioned the inn and the few two-story houses along the main street of the village, the onlookers began counting their prayer beads and changed their usual form of meditation. The horsemen flanking the purple palanquin of the high functionary shouted orders at the armed subalterns, and the commotion ceased. A curse had just fallen upon the Emperor's representative but he suspected nothing at all. Soon after, violent squalls followed by snowfall immobilized the delegation, and an inky black sky loomed menacingly. As soon as he had settled into his quarters, the mandarin began to sense that his presence was not welcome in this forsaken place. The elements were set loose, and although he asked the monks at the monastery courteously, no one seemed to know of this novice, and even less the subject of her philosophical meetings. The search seemed to have come to a dead end. Before long, however, a few dozen soldier monks clustered around an incredibly beautiful girl with a shaven head. She was dressed in nomad's clothes, half-hidden in a large sheepskin overcoat trimmed with snow leopard fur. She held coral prayer beads in her right hand and wore boots on her feet. Spotting her, the mandarin came out onto the balcony of his residence, as if he wanted to talk to her. But in a flash, the girl raised her hand in his direction and the high functionary was transformed into a multitude of tiny multicolored rags which scattered in an instant and were carried away by the gusts of wind. In the distance a horse whinnied, and the mandarin's party—terrified by what they had witnessed—ran off in confusion, never to return. And thus, as legend has it, the symbol of the wind horse came into being for the very first time.

FESTIVAL
DAYS

FROM
DAY TO DAY

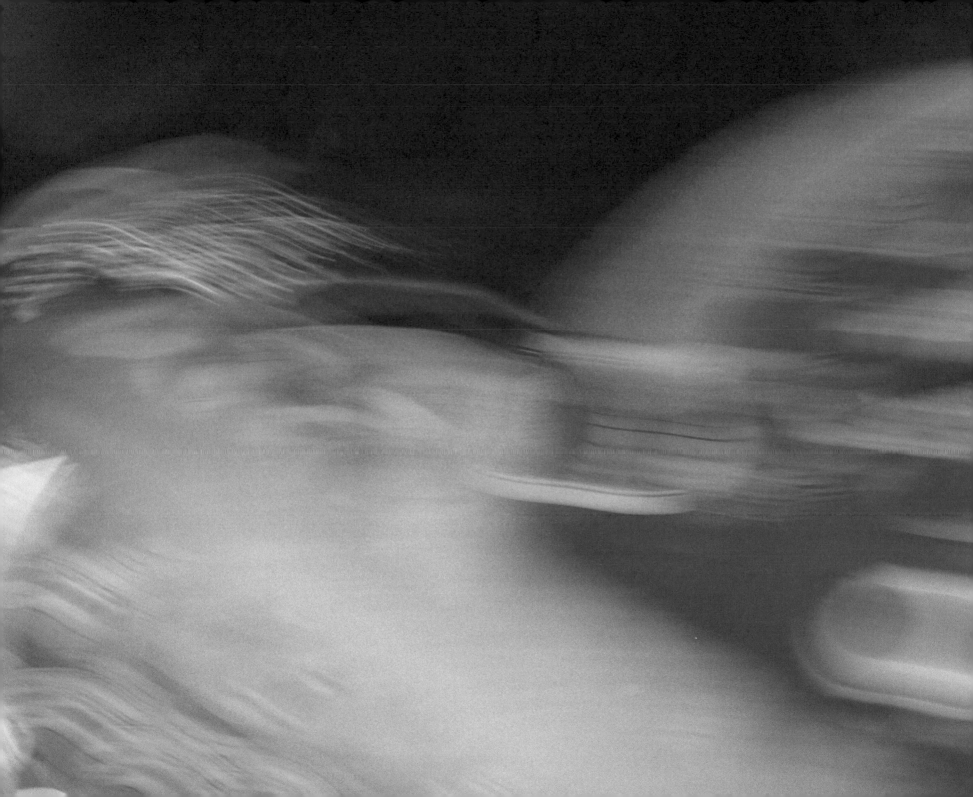

OM MANI PEME HUNG The sky is blue in Tibet but the tensions remain the same; as everywhere else, the different nomadic tribes that make up the landscape have lived and worked together for such a long time. Muslim Tibetans are shopkeepers; the nomads are herdsmen; the monasteries offer spiritual life; and the young people wear designer sunglasses and strut around with cell phones in hand.

OM MANI PEME HUNG The gods are to be found everywhere in Tibet, and although Buddhism and Lamaism dominate, this does not mean that ancient beliefs have been abandoned. The wind possesses a power that demands more than just respect; thus, prayers and votive offerings must be offered up. These are written on scraps of material, which can be either scattered to the winds or tied together so that the breeze, blowing through them, can carry them up to heaven and beyond to the farthest regions of the galaxy.

Accordingly, he who binds up his wishes has a chance of seeing them come true, and if a storm whips up and carries the message far away then this will bring good luck. The prayer flags, called wind horses, that flap noisily high up on steep paths and on the mountainsides are prayers addressed directly to the elements.

May the gods be with you, little man, and may harmony rule the course of your life under the care of the compassionate Buddha.

OM MANI PEME HUNG This is a different Tibet—far removed from the urban West's idea of Buddhism—where the flapping wind horses bear messages dedicated to the gods and to life. It possesses nothing of the hypocrisy of Western made-to-measure images, which offer a reassuring depiction of a Tibet where men fly kites and practice archery in village festivals, and stick out their tongue as a sign of satisfaction, while monks do nothing but chant and pray like children in an environment that is harsh, perhaps, but so superficially charming.

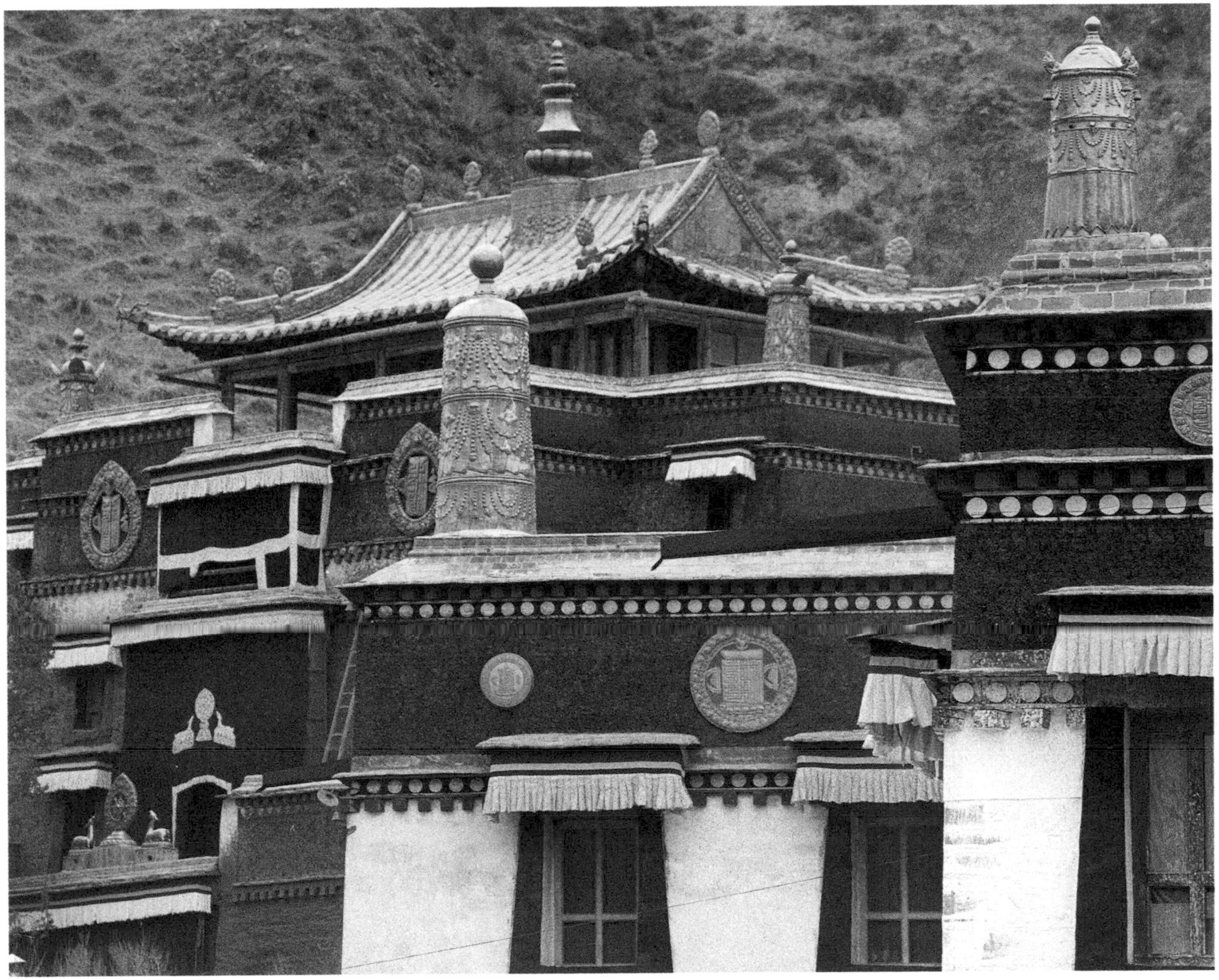

OM MANI PEME HUNG The monks' silhouettes are draped in every shade from the spectrum of red—from crimson through an infinite number of variations to pale pink. Barefoot inside their boots despite the intense cold, some have the look of a *condottiere*, inspiring more fear by the power they can exert than respect due to all their mantras dedicated to inner peace and detachment.

✛ ✛ ✛ ✛ ✛ ✛ ✛ ✛ ✛ ✛ ✛ ✛ ✛ ✛ ✛ ✛ ✛ ✛

OM MANI PEME HUNG To struggle is also to understand, to be smart. The monasteries often look like fortresses, and while spirituality constitutes a priority there, a comfortable way of life does not. Money, technical progress, and the temptations of extreme consumerism have emerged on the caravan routes. But the Tibetan people in all their diversity must not be abandoned to climbers and trekkers from the world over.

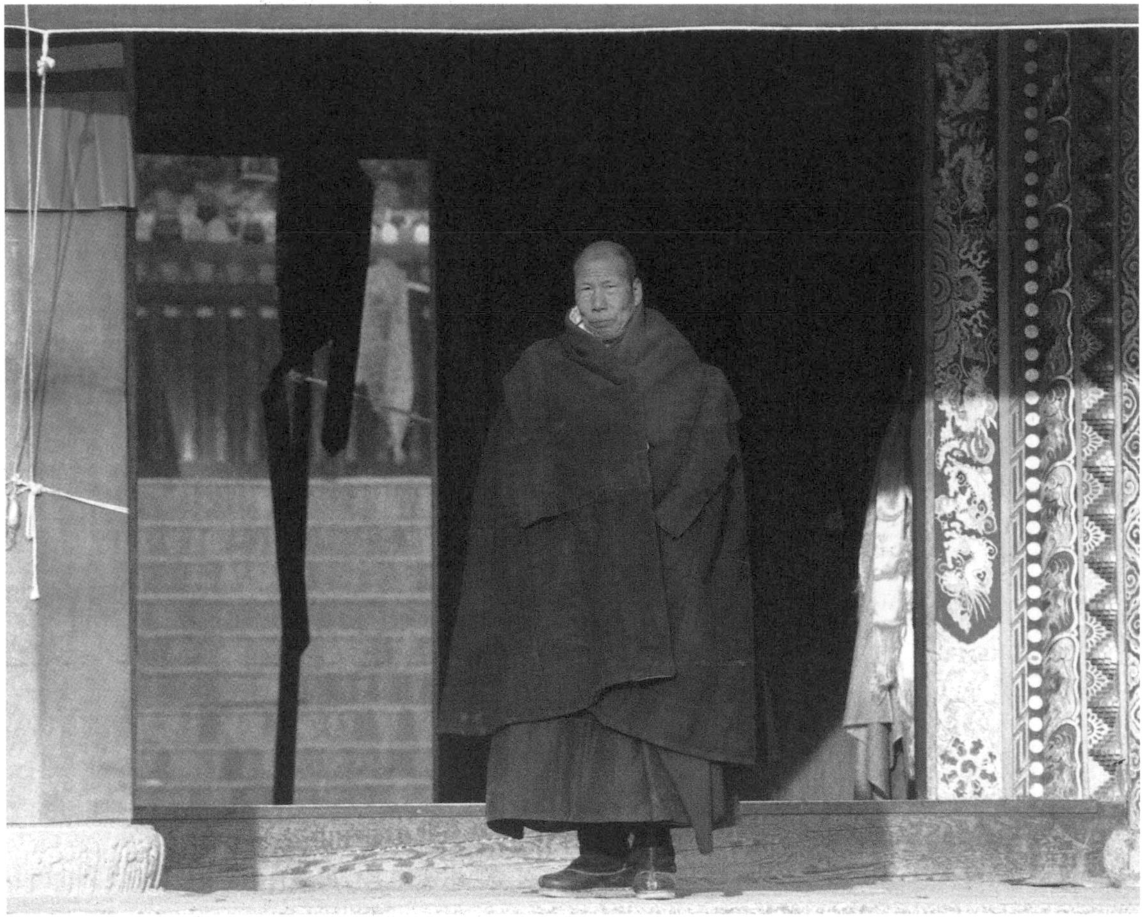

OM MANI PEME HUNG May they have long life and may the gods watch over their destinies. The goal of a peaceful future seems a long way off in this immense country. His Holiness the fourteenth Dalai Lama preaches nonviolence within the Buddhist philosophy but also as an actor on the twenty-first-century international stage.

✝ ✝ ✝ ✝ ✝ ✝ ✝ ✝ ✝ ✝ ✝ ✝ ✝ ✝ ✝ ✝

EDITORIAL DIRECTION

Suzanne Tise-Isoré
Collection Styles & Design

DESIGN

Bernard Lagacé
Nils Herrmann

TRANSLATED FROM THE FRENCH BY

Philippa Hurd

COPYEDITING

Helen Adedotun

EDITORIAL ASSISTANTS

Frédérique Lagache
Delphine Montagne

COLOR SEPARATION

Les artisans du Regard

Distributed in North America
by Rizzoli International Publications, Inc.

Simultaneously published in French as *Beauté nomade*
© Flammarion, 2006
English-language edition
© Flammarion, 2006

Flammarion
87, quai Panhard et Levassor
75647 Paris Cedex 13
www.editions.flammarion.com

FC0536-06-IX
ISBN-10: 2-0803-0536-0
ISBN-13: 9782080305367
Dépôt légal: 06/2006
Printed in Singapore by Tien Wah Press